Signs in action

FINE ARTS
Carnegie Education Center
Carnegie-Mellon University

Signs in action

James Sutton

Studio Vista: London
Reinhold Publishing Corporation: New York

Cover photo Herbert Spencer

Photo p.1 Crosby Fletcher Forbes and Gill

The author is grateful to Alan Bartran, David Warner and Herbert Spencer for their generous help with this book.

Signs in action
A Studio Vista/Reinhold Art Paperback
edited by John Lewis
© James Sutton 1965
Published in London by Studio Vista Limited
Blue Star House, Highgate Hill, London N19
and in New York by Reinhold Publishing Corporation
430 Park Avenue, New York
Library of Congress Catalog Card Number 65-24058
Set in 9/12 Univers Medium 689
Printed in the Netherlands
by N.V. Drukkerij Koch & Knuttel, Gouda

ph

Introduction

Signs, though linked to both architecture and typography, are a separate field of design. They offer wide opportunities for lively and original work, but it is still a rather neglected field. Signs are less permanent than buildings, they receive little care in design, and no school provides any specific training for architectural lettering. If such a course existed it would have to insist on the primary considerations of function common to most modern design disciplines. It would also have to stress the importance of exploiting the opportunities presented by the site, for though road and traffic signs may well have to follow definite, fortunately recognizable formulae, the signs of commerce have no such limitations. Here there are pleas for brashness or good manners, for architectural or anti-architectural signs.

Apart from the special possibilities and limitations of letterforms, there are the infinite variations of spacing and positioning to be considered. The signs may reflect current typographic practice — indeed signs must be very much of the moment to look fresh and have strong impact. Typeface letterforms may be the currently accepted form for the alphabet. But merely to enlarge typeforms gives signs a flimsy, weak appearance, often quite ineffective in the street, where a strong active line and form would give letters the power to relate to their architectural setting, and to hold their own against the traffic noise, lights and movement and other distractions of the street.

factors that make signs effective is an important aspect to sign design

The signmaker has two jobs: to put the literal message across as directly as possible, and to devise a form which is suitable for the best expression of the message, with regard to its literal content, and architectural setting. Often the way people say things tells one far more than the words alone. So too with signs. Many signs are illegible, yet attractive and full of expression; many more are legible, but hideous. The designer's problem of function and form becomes, for the spectator, 'have I understood, and do I like what I have understood?' (or 'do I obey what I have understood?' if the sign message requires action).

Italian kilometre stone
Photo Alan Bartram

Road sign in southern Italy
Photo Herbert Spencer

Wooden sign with painted letters, near Waterhouses,
County Durham
Photo David Warner

Here is a kilometre stone; the principle message is that it is 319 kilometres to Rome, which is not very useful information perhaps, but the road number and the distance to Lucera are also given clearly; the appearance of the whole is very pleasant, with good, if somewhat small lettering, wholly appropriate in the wide, empty Apulian countryside. Together with the three black and white stone bollards, it is typical of the grand yet unpretentious way Italians design for highways, or for anything else.

A cryptic message here, but if you are confident of your road, and know the name of the next major town (which has probably already been indicated), it is all that you need. The less said, the clearer the message, and the choice of these numerals gives the sign great charm as well as authority.

A simple sign in the Durham countryside. It is direct yet very expressive. Such simplicity is rare.

Mile post in stone and cast iron, Sussex
Photo Herbert Spencer

Top Left:
Mile post in stone, painted black and white Trumpington, Cambridge
Photo Herbert Spencer

Mile post in cast iron, Isle of Mull
Photo Herbert Spencer

Milestones from Cambridge, Sussex, Yorkshire and the Isle of Mull. What could show more clearly the Englishness of England, or the Scottishness of Scotland? The first is, in fact, using a Roman numeral; it is two miles, not eleven, from Cambridge. Fanciful, delicate or clumsy they are delightful as objects, with a hearty disdain for function and discipline. Can their virtues apply today? Can design in these foggy islands be more logical and clearly expressed and yet keep a national quality? The problem is not easy. The alternative is to follow, however reluctantly and inadequately, American and European leadership.

Mile post in stone, painted black and white, Richmond, Yorkshire
Photo Herbert Spencer

The earnest attempt to give contemporary punch to polite signwriter's Roman by means of a holy trademark is poor signposting and bad advertising.

Sign painted on tin-plate sheet, Guildford
Photo David Warner

Dutch road signs between Rotterdam and the airport
Photos Margaret Wissing

We are getting into heavier traffic here, and the relaxed manner appropriate to the countryside is no longer permissable.

On fast, busy motorways clarity, order, consistency and authority are required. Road signs must be clear, easily and quickly understood, and look as if they mean business. Painting them on the road is logical, this is where the driver should be looking, and it reduces roadside clutter. The obvious point of positioning signs to the spectator's best advantage is curiously often overlooked.

It is not the purpose of this book to advance a theory for road signs. As with most design problems, the best solutions come from a clear unbiassed look at the needs of the job, and from deftness and discipline in meeting them. Directional, warning, admonitory or informatory signs clearly have a distinct but related job to do. This must be evident in the design of the lettering and in the colour and shape (particularly for the colour-blind) of the sign. One symbol could replace many signs which consist of a confusing arrangement of words. Where unrelated, illegible styles are used together, a clear, well-designed alphabet would make sense of dangerous, ineffective nonsense. But careless placing and bad letter and word spacing can make signs in related styles equally confusing.

Common sense is a prized national characteristic, but we make sparing use of it in design, and we take an arrogant delight in our blindness to matters of style. Yet without intelligence and visual sensitivity, design is neither effective nor attractive.

The recent decision in Great Britain to

plement the recommendations of the Woroys Committee has meant that for road signs e approved standard Grotesque letter (sans rif), with its carefully written manual conlling spacing, sizes and layout, is now to place our current collection of oddities.

is decision has resulted from a long, detailed, ientific study of the needs of road users in day's conditions. Consideration of the aesthes of the colours and scale of the signs has en given proper importance. However the w signs must be positioned sensibly, and exing clutter removed with equal care and ergy.

r most purposes miniscule (lower case) ters are to be preferred to capitals. This has en a growing preference since the early 30s, when the Bauhaus published the theory that capitals were an unnecessary and obsolete form for the alphabet.

A word makes a unique and distinctive shape in small letters, but a dull rectangle in capitals —

england / ENGLAND.

The free, irregular shapes of small letters and words suit our general preference for the lively and informal. But we are used to capitals for place names — certainly for the initial letter — and the formal, static quality of capitals has a functional use for road signs. 'London' is easier to identify than 'LONDON', but 'LONDON' tells you you've arrived. Similarly 'GET IN LANE' can look like a place-name: 'get in lane' is read faster, and looks like a command: *'get in lane'* (condensed italics) is more urgent still, but lacks authority, and is not so legible.

Marble Arch, London
Photo Herbert Spencer

German street sign
Photo David Lock and Terry Smith

Safety for 50,000,000 motor vehicles is not material helped by this confused 'Christmas Tree' of signs downtown Washington DC
Photo United States Information Service

These monstrous Christmas Trees are confusing difficult to read and hideous. An ill co-ordinate mass of verbiage.

Is every sign on p. 16 necessary? If the author ities tidied up the mess, the driver could see clearly, one sign. Even two or three co-ordinate signs supporting rather than fighting each othe – or repeating the message – can be effective but completely different signs saying the same thing can never be.

How it can be done.

Painted wood sign, Cortina, Italy ▶
Photo Publifoto Milan

Road Junction, Hammersmith, London
Photo David Warner

16

Sign on the M6
Photo Press Association Photos Ltd

The New Traffic Signs in Great Britain

Since the Worboys report was published in Great Britain in 1963 the Ministry of Transport has issued one small booklet which differs in some respects from the Worboys recommendations. This is no doubt inevitable – the scheme is bound to have teething troubles – but in the meantime a number of new signs conflict with both. And the Ministry of Transport has yet to publish its manuals for the design of directional and mandatory signs. *The Manual of Informatory Signs* is available, but unless all three are published and properly distributed there are bound to be wide differences of interpretation of existing instructions.

Although a very much improved system, the new signs have certain features which make for ineffective communication: the signs are of three different kinds – symbols, words and pictures; the designs are of different weights, which results in the 'bold' signs looking more urgent or important than the 'light' versions; the signs with words have far less impact than the ones with symbols; the 'no entry, one way street' sign is far larger and stronger than all the others. There is some doubt as to whether the Transport Letter designed by Jock Kinneir is quite as suitable as the more elegant Dutch letter. Its weighty design seems better for rail traffic than for motor roads. The great width and size of the M6 sign and the relationship of map and places names make the message difficult to take in easily at a glance.

The new square arrows are a departure from the pointed ones in use on the M1 – the change was made because of greater legibility at speed, but the new ones look very static.

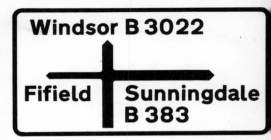

Advance direction sign for cross roads junction of non-primary routes

Secondary advance direction sign for an intermediate junction on motorway

Direction sign to Motorway for use on non-primary roads using the light alphabet

The square arrow on non-primary roads
Pointed arrow on motorway exit sign

End of temporary obstruction

Sign to direct traffic to the motorway

Traffic signs for motorways and all-purpose roads in use in Great Britain using letters designed by Jock Kinneir

No U turns

Capital letters carry authority

Slippery road

Direction sign for use on non-primary roads
using the bold alphabet

No entry : the most dominant of city street signs

Road works

Direction signs to lavatories

19

Arrows in a brick road, Amsterdam
Photo Herbert Spencer

A road of arrows.

Corrugated sign, Park Lane, London
Photo Herbert Spencer

This rough and ready arrow is surprisingly subtle and effective. The ripple of the corrugated iron and the curves of the arrow-head give the message life, urgency and elegance.

Garage sign, West London
Photo Herbert Spencer

This shy little notice hopes it will not attract too much attention. It is outside a filling station on a busy road. It would be more at home pointing to fresh eggs and cut flowers in a country lane.

Garage sign, West London
Photo Herbert Spencer

The ugly petrol sign is clearer and more urgent
than the confused warning sign above it. This
tries to inform, warn and advertise all at once,
but does nothing effectively. How much better
an exclamation mark would have been. The
petrol sign is straightforward and to the point,
and the white space round the lettering gives
added punch and clarity.

COLORADO SPEED LIMITS
NARROW MOUNTAIN HIGHWAY...20 M.P.H.
OPEN MOUNTAIN HIGHWAY......40 M.P.H.
OPEN COUNTRY HIGHWAY......60 M.P.H.
COLORADO STATE HIGHWAY DEPARTMENT

Sign, Colorado
Photos United States Information Service

Harbor Freeway
Downtown

99 Santa Ana Frwy
66 Hollywood Frwy

Freeway sign, California
Photo United States Information Service

Painted sign, 's-Hertogenbosch, Holland
Photo Herbert Spencer

Letterforms well suited to the brick surface. The design shows care and sensibility, and yet avoids fuss and pomposity. It would have worked less well had the direction of the arrow not been the same as the direction of reading.

Devilish clever these Chinese! Only a grand master could have turned this simple job into a tortuous puzzle. The complicated shapes and the spineless, uncommanding lettering also help to make this a perfect example of what to avoid. It evokes only too poignantly the earlier New Towns in Britain.

VEHICLE
ENTRY
←
DEEPFIELD
ROAD

Sign at Bracknell
Photo Herbert Spencer

Painted sign
Photo Herbert Spencer

Here, under heavy fire from motorists confused
by the previous sign, the owner has desper-
ately written a message with the nearest tool
to hand, a spray-gun.

Cement wall, Seahouses, Northumberland
Photo David Warner

The same message, but part of a grander design.
A notice which is a painting which is a wall.

Sign, London
Photo Herbert Spencer

Signs that give orders must look as if they mean
to be obeyed. This one looks as if it would stand
no argument, despite the peeling paint. Here is
a burly, all-seeing foreman speaking, with a
wide range of swear-words ready for those who
don't bother to listen.

These three weedy specimens, on the other hand, look like an unfortunate schoolmaster who knows he has no hope whatever of controlling his class.

Sign, Knightsbridge, London
Photo Herbert Spencer

The function of directional signs — to lead con
fidently, authoritatively, swiftly and safely to
destination — applies to pedestrian notices a
well as to those for vehicles. The pedestrian get
little help from this collection, apparently de
signed to reduce him to a state of nervous in
decision. When new signs are added thought
lessly they cancel each other out.

Sign, Park Lane, London
Photo Herbert Spencer

Here the urgency is alarming !

Stove enamelled sign, Düsseldorf
Photo David Lock and Terry Smith

31

West London Air Terminal
Design (Christopher Timings) Design Research Unit
photo David Warner

The lettering on this hanging sign (top left) is satisfactory, but the arrangement of words makes reading difficult. The unrelated buffet sign should be scrapped, and the message incorporated on the other sign.

The signposting of airports, terminals, stations, hospitals, universities, and any other complex building involving the correct, orderly movement of vehicles and people, is similar to the problem of road signs. The importance of clarity and unambiguity is not usually due to actual danger arising through misdirection, but because people in these buildings are often anxious and tense. Any scheme of signposting that creates a feeling of confidence and reassurance, as well as imposing control, is doing its job.

Euston Station, London
photos David Warner

33

West London Air Terminal
Design and photo Design Research Unit (Christopher Timings)

London Airport
Design and photo Crosby Fletcher Forbes and Gill ▶

This example shows careful thought and dis
ciplined execution.
Too many 'helpful' signs defeat their own pur
pose. The architecture of the building shoul
indicate the flow of vehicles and movement, s
that few signs are needed. Here are some ex
amples of how this can be done.

A beautifully designed set of indicator boards in a shop. They are clear, well-proportioned orderly and simple.

Spanish excursion boat timetable ▶
Photo Herbert Spencer

Hardly an example of how to inform clearly ir four languages. However, in a relaxed holiday mood one can enjoy the texture produced by these excellent Spanish stencil letters.

Habitat, Brompton Road, London
Design Conran Design Group
Photo David Warner

Building Site, Notting Hill Gate, London
Photo David Warner

The Air Ministry stencil letters are decorativ too, but much too demure for their purpose. I is interesting to compare these examples with the Italian km stone on p. 8.

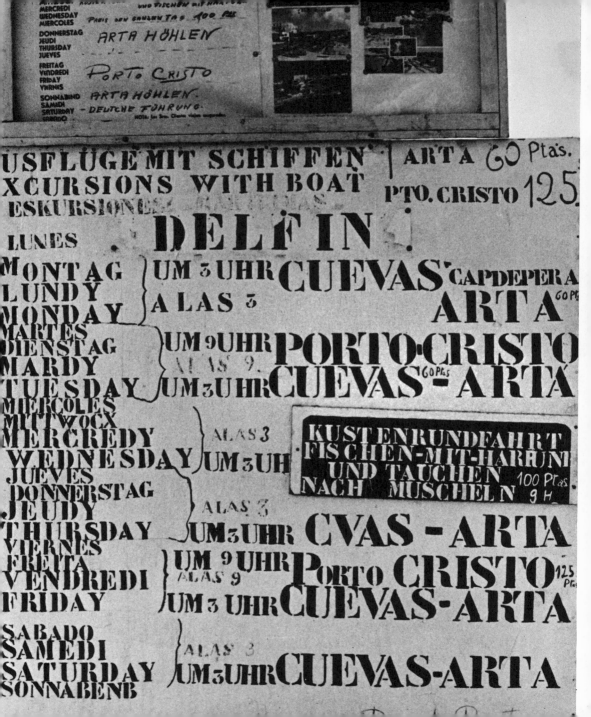

· NOTICE ·

Visitors are reminded that many of the Trees are Old, and liable to shed branches without warning.

Windsor Great Park
Photo Herbert Spencer

Russell Square, London ▶
Photo David Warner

Informal, royally-relaxed lettering, which per
fectly reflects the park atmosphere, particularl
when phrased with unhurried courtesy and
ending with unexpected menace. Worthy o
George III in his last years, or at least of thos
unsung heroes the sign-writers and letter
cutters of his reign.

Another pleasantly parkish notice, painted
white on grey, though the deck chair notice
ought to have been incorporated properly with
the rest of the lettering.

**RUSSELL
SQUARE**

Dont leave
litter

Persons with dogs are
required to keep them
under proper control

DECK CHAIRS
CHARGE 3ᴰ PER SESSION

Cast iron sign, Stafford
Photo Herbert Spencer

Black and white ceramic tile sign, Hampstead, London
Photo David Warner

Cast iron painted sign, Leeds
Photo Herbert Spencer

Chiswick, London
Photo Herbert Spencer

Place Montbenon, Lausanne
Photo Herbert Spencer

Which street would you prefer to live in? One of the three opposite, or Rivercourt Road? The latter is clear, reasonably well-spaced and designed, with decent letterforms, but the others make up for comparative illegibility by their personal quality. And this, in quiet, small roads where people live, is more important. Inappropriate on the highway, they are right here. The appeal of the Swiss sign is not wholly due to the way it evokes holidays in Switzerland; its chunky urbanity is more human, less anonymous, than the similarly produced Rivercourt Road sign.

Now we are well into the town. Whereas in the countryside and on motorways there should be few signs, in towns and cities they are a frequent and desirable feature. Streets are full of them; taken together they make streets look like streets. They can be of any material — whitewashed, they will stay there till it rains; cut in stone, they will often outlast the building. They can make living in towns an endless source of pleasure, amusement and discovery. Or they can wreck a building or a street, and shout vicious insults in an environment which cannot absorb them. At night they can completely change a city. Often seen, but not looked at, they cannot be ignored by anyone interested in modern townscape, advertising, or by town-dwellers who mind, consciously or not, about the places in which they live and work.

Signs can be designed as part of the building — thought of as an essential part of its form — shop signs and fascias, or even posters.

The commonest fault today in sign designing, unheard of before this century, is merely to enlarge a typeface. For most signs this is not enough, and for architectural signs it can be disastrous. Even a good typeface makes a bad architectural sign, and the special limitations of form and spacing imposed by printing techniques are irrelevant in sign-writing. Instead, new disciplines and greater opportunities for freedom and originality could give this field of design a unique quality, especially when the possibilities of three-dimensional letters in new materials have been considered. An unwitting accomplice in the missuse of type has been the *Architectural Review*. Its exciting, uninhibited and zestful use of type is excellent for a magazine, so long as legibility does not

suffer; but its architect readers seldom realis that what looks good on paper is weak an awkward eighteen inches high, carved in ston cut out of sheet metal or plastic, or moulde into solid forms against a concrete wall twent feet above eye-level.

In many cases the architect, shopfitter and clier prefer to leave the whole matter in the hands c the sign manufacturer. The results of this lazy cynical irresponsibility is glaringly obvious i every street in the country. At worst it mean misguided attempts to make lettering on com plicated plastic, metal and illuminated sign conform to classical inscriptions (see your loca bank for an example); at best it means adoptin styles made popular at the Festival of Britai which, together with the Festival's architectura influence, has resulted in signs like leaflets an buildings like stage sets — flat and flimsy, self conscious or coy. One looks back with nostalgi not only to the nineteenth century, when desig ners had invincible confidence, but also to th nineteen-thirties, when so much serious an original work was done.

Shop signs and fascia boards are advertisin within architectural limits. These limits are se by the style of the shop front and the pattern o the shops in the street. To make a shop from look right is more a question of weight an filling a space than one of style of letterform If the weight is wrong, the design looks wea and half-hearted; if the name doesn't fit th area allotted to it, the building looks as if it need shoring up. A shop is a glass-fronted bo: divided into verticals and horizontals by struc tural elements like posts and beams, door anc glazing bars. If the beam across the top which keeps the building up is shown as a fascia board, the letters on that board must look as strong as the beam behind it. This works well as a frame for the goods in the window, and suggests that the shopkeeper is there for good and is not going to close down tomorrow.

The second way of dealing with shops is to treat the glass box as a separate unit, existing in its own right, independent of the house above it. This can be done by running a long canopy above a row of shop units, so that from the pavement the building above is screened off or lost in darkness.

Thus the shop can set its own pattern, quite unrelated to weighty, load-bearing architectural elements. The designer can use a variety of styles and letterforms, as if he were laying out an advertisement or a poster.

The Civic Trust schemes have resulted in some startling improvements. But too much chasteness in street signs is worse than vulgarity. Spontaneity and vigour are lost where standards are imposed from above. Their plaque, 'designed within the office', is a poor advertisement for their judgement and has something in common with the new town arrow. Street signs should be chosen less from a desire to show 'good taste' than from a wish to do a particular job as effectively as possible; and this involves consideration for one's neighbours and the streetscape. If signmakers offered their customers as many stock letters as were evidently available fifty years ago, they would have a chance of choosing the best. As it is, the more materials and techniques available, the less thought and invention is given to appropriate letterforms.

Overleaf :

A collection of wiry shapes by day becomes a scene of feverish movement by night, creating bizarre pools of colour, turning people momentarily magenta or emerald, shattering pompous stone daytime facades into gay, ever-changing cascades of brilliant colour and spiky shapes.

Cast aluminium sign
Photo Civic Trust

43

Commercial Road, London
Photo David Warner

Wardour Street, London
Photo David Warner

his is war — against the street. Warner-Pathé rides down its block shouting 'keep off, this ours.' Worse still is the garage and its assem- ly of unco-ordinated signs, notices and ban- ers. The garage above dominates a longer section of road than Warner-Pathé, but how much more sympathetically. And how much tidier it is than the garage opposite. (Even AGIP garages in England, however, are spoilt by tatty signs, afterthoughts and dirty clutter.)

An example of the work of the Civic Trust.
spite of the best of intentions, more is lost tha
gained by this over-dainty, dull redesigning.

Euston Arch 1830 (lettering 1870)
Photo Civic Trust

From sign-making in a street context we proceed to signs as part of the building. Euston Arch, recently destroyed by British Railways, was a splendid example. Although added forty years after the arch was built, the letters are anything but an afterthought, they complete the design. Clear and legible, the letters demonstrate the triumphant pride in themselves and their achievements that the men of the Railway Age were justified in feeling. The everyday problems of what to say, and where and how to say it, are all majestically solved here.

Columbus Haus, Berlin 1931
Photos courtesy Ralph Beyer

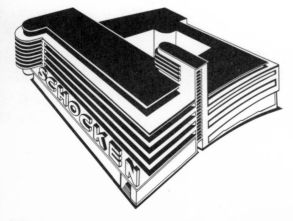

Among modern architects Eric Mendelsohn wa
rare in making use of lettering in the design c
buildings right from the earliest sketches. Sign
were used as an architectural element in h
designs — as tough and purposeful as the stee
glass and concrete of the structure.

Schocken Department Store, Chemnitz, Germany 192

Schocken Department Store, Stuttgart 1928

Here is a recent attempt, where unfortunatel something went wrong between design and ex ecution. The E and D on the side of the buildin are based on different founts of type, and th numerals have poor scale and position. Bu more use of lettering in similar ways woul transform many office buildings in this countr

Elder Dempster building, Lagos
Photos James Cubbitt

Architecture of Technology Exhibition, London South Bank
Architect Theo Crosby
Lettering Edward Wright
Photos Edward Wright and John French

Edward Wright's lettering for the *Architecture of Technology* exhibition is a superb example of lettering used as advertising, decoration and information. It is also a pyrotechnical display in four languages.

The close up shows how, due to the wall construction of loaned scaffolding planks (which could not be sawn to size), the lettering had to accept and overcome the irregularities of the surface.

Galt's toy factory, Cheadle, Cheshire
Design Ken Garland
Photo Ralph Marshall

Galt's toyshop, Great Marlborough Street, London
Design Ken Garland, Photos David Warner and John Maltby

Lettering sensitively and sensibly added to an existing building. The tough nineteenth-century Cheshire warehouses have been allowed to remain themselves, complemented by equally forthright but refined lettering. An excellent example of a sign closely relating to the building, and making its effect with precision and style.

The toy factory's London shop. What appears to be rather questionable nonsense on the extreme left, works triumphantly when its vital corner position is realized.

University of East Anglia, Norwich
Design and photo Herbert Spencer

University signs. All things change. Arts degrees give way to science, Trajan Roman to Grot, and the stonemason to the typographic designer. Though most typefaces are quite unsuitable as models for architectural lettering, the Grots, old and modern, provide a perfectly adequate basis for such signs as the one on the left. In the change from printed word to painted sign, spacing can be adjusted and letters subtly modified.

55

Motel, Cortina, Italy
Photo Publifoto Milan

Simple lettering that is extremely considerate
towards its fine building. Another example of
an unlittered garage, and one that in fact has a
large number of signs, without appearing sordid
and depressing. Contrast the pictures opposite.

Motel sign
Photo United States Information Service

56

Motel, Camden, New Jersey
Photo United States Information Service

St Paul's Church, Bow Common, London 1959
Architects Robert Maguire and Keith Murray
Lettering Ralph Beyer (carved in chipboard and cast in concrete)
Photo Norman Gold

In this interesting modern English church the spare geometry of the structure is balanced and complemented by Ralph Beyer's humane, highly personal lettering.

Druce, Baker Street, London, carved in granite and gilded
photos David Warner

Two more signs that consider their buildings — Druce is good and strong; the name becomes a trademark rather than a word to be read. Peter Robinson, in a rather similar context, shows how to create a striking identity using architectural letters and remaining perfectly readable. Note how the sharp corners become lost at night.

Peter Robinson, Strand, London
Architect Denys Lasdun
Design Edward Wright
photos David Warner

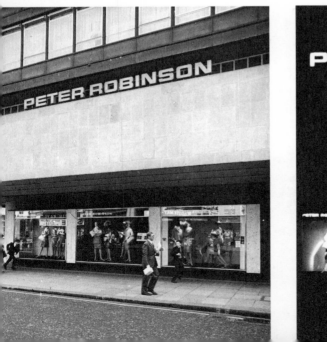

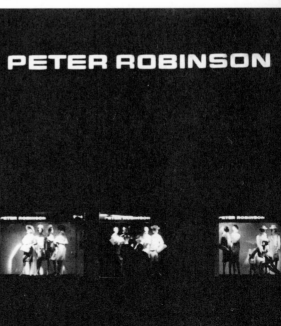

Pub, Guildford
Photo David Warner

The Astolat — spiky typeforms in a fidgety arrangement. Contrast it with the vigour of form and arrangement on The Three Tuns or The Queen, where the lettering appears to have grown out from the wall.

Gardners is a piece of outrage against the street — King's Road Chelsea. The gross letterform (though hardly bigger than The Queen), demon strate the fatal influence of the typesheet on mannerless designer with no sense of scale

Supermarket, Kings Road, Chelsea, London
Photo David Warner

Wooden letters, gilded, Durham
photo David Warner

Wooden letters, painted, Bradford (now demolished)
photo Herbert Spencer

Another example of a perversely chosen type face (so many others would have been les bad) stuck down like a stamp on an envelope. Even the Cock Hotel, using a rather better ver sion of this letter and on the kind of building mor suited to it, has spoilt the effect by using italics If lettering is part of the design of a building, a it certainly is here, it *must* echo the stability an structural feel of the architecture. This need b no means restrict the designer – the two sign opposite have been moulded with apparent art lessness, almost independently of the building They are free, organic forms, contrasting wit the structure, yet relating subtly to it. A growt on the wall surface, they do not sugges instability.

Euston Road, London
Photo David Warner

Hotel sign, Epping
Photo Herbert Spence

Garage sign, Stafford
Photo Herbert Spencer

Hardware store, Ireland
Photo Herbert Spencer

Basle
Photos Lawrence Carey

Co-ordinated schemes of shop names need not lack variety and vigour; this series at Basle, meticulously carried out in a common material, gives each shop its own character — original yet legible, these shop names are clearly visible yet keep their place.

Hille, Albemarle Street, London
Design Ivan Dodd, Photo David Warner

An isolated box jutting out into the street, the Hille sign relates well with the building, and makes a dramatic eye-catcher like a packing case being slowly hoisted to an upper floor of a warehouse.

Hille, Manchester
Design Ivan Dodd
Photo John Mills

National Commercial Bank of Scotland, Georgie Road,
Edinburgh
Photo A. G. Ingram

A bank in a quiet Edinburgh street, and its
branch near Piccadilly Circus. Both signs are
appropriate to their surroundings and to their
buildings. The Edinburgh branch's lettering
looks well against the rough gritty stone sur-
faces, and the modern roman V-cut in polished
granite suits the large expensive city office.

National Commercial Bank of Scotland, Haymarket,
London SWI
Design James Sutton, Photo John Maltby

Pub, Barbican, City of London
Photo David Warner

e!

he Type Vie
es may wor
ents or sugge

Pub,   ate, London
Photo

Bazaa   lge Green, London
Photo

Ano   sign. What is the building? A
banl   l chapel or a crematorium? It's
a 'p   The Podium! Another pub using
a la   n a Festival of Britain typeface
has   in a strident yet inert facade.
Wit   ascia it would be an attractive
building.

By mounting this ebullient, dashing sign inside
the shop window, Bazaar have made a striking
effect and the street has not suffered.

French Government Tourist Office, Piccadilly, London
Design Erno Goldfinger Photo, David Warner

Belgian Government Tourist Office, Haymarket, London
Photo David Warner

A clever sign for the French Government Tourist Office enlivens the street without destroying it. A smaller variant, below, becomes an intriguing game.

Opposite:
A bit of fun for a shop selling Victorian furniture — Tuscan letters carved in wood and gilded.

A bit of depression from a shipping line. The letters are coarse and corpulent — their italic lurch has a shattering effect on the building, a vital structural beam is knocked sideways, and the whole street is consequently in peril.

Antique shop, Kings Road, Chelsea, London
Design James Sutton
Photo David Warner

Shipping office, Bond Street, London
Photo David Warner

Chicago skyline
Photos Alan Fletcher

These Chicago signs make the skyline exciting and are as much urban architecture as the factory chimney. The law forbids breaking the skyline with signs in England – though not in Europe – but these two examples show two ways of dramatically floating letters in space.

Opposite:
Beautiful signs from Habitat. Typeforms used with imagination and a sure sense of scale. This beautiful nineteenth-century example painted on a wire gauze screen shows the difference in disciplines between type design and signwriting.

Habitat, Brompton Road,
London
Design Conran Design Group
Photo David Warner

Solicitors, Hanover Street,
London
Photo David Warner

entmakers, Old Kent Road,
ecorated for the Coronation
hoto Civic Trust

These pleasing examples are each suited to its building and type of shop. Sutherland's shop shows the Civic Trust at their best. Edgington shows how to cheer up a street yet be a good businessman as well. This shows it *is* possible to attract attention and be gay and pleasant about it.

Overleaf:

Exploiting materials brings dividends. Such accidents are a vital part of streetscape, and if not to be contrived, can be assisted.

Voburn Walk, Bloomsbury, London
hoto David Warner

entish Town, London
hoto David Warner

Marlborough Court, Carnaby Street, London WI
hoto David Warner

Art Nouveau, Amsterdam
Photo Herbert Spencer

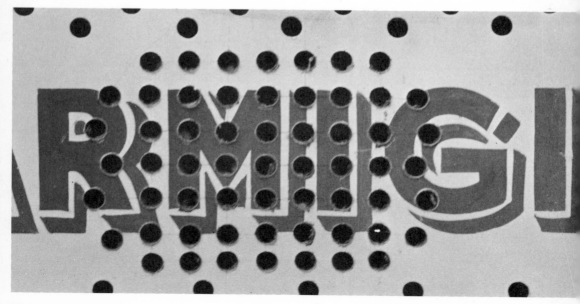

South Kensington London
Photo Herbert Spencer

The effect of materials
Photos Robert Brownjohn

Oyster bar, City of London
Photos David Warner

Signs can take on a life of their own. Parts fa
off, are reflected, cast shadows, repeat them
selves, get strange neighbours, become reverse
or distorted (as when seen through plain
reeded glass), or, if done on flexible material, g
folded, twisted. Many of these chance effec
could be deliberately achieved in the design
shopwindows, and the ideas which hithert
have been used in the design of neon signs a
very dull and ordinary when one considers th
possibilities suggested by this dramatical
exciting medium.

Bank, Lombard Street, London
Photo David Warner

anging signs. By their position these could be
ne most noticeable signs in the street. They are
ne oldest form of advertising, dating back to
oman trade and guild signs, the precursors of
eraldry. The strong geometric forms and the
imple, vividly alive symbols of birds and ani-
nals have as much relevance today as they had
nen for the purpose of quick identification and
isual communication. In the eighteenth century
anging signs were the standard practice, and
ascia boards are a recent arrival, perhaps partly
ue to legal restriction on hanging signs, and
lso to Victorian status-consciousness. It looks
rander to have 'footware SAMUEL SNOD-
RASS specialist' on the fascia than no name
nd a wooden hunting boot, four-feet tall and
overed in gold leaf, swinging on an iron brac-
et. Some of the signs that survive are timid and
ussy. The 'sun' on the next page shows how a
ood symbol boldly designed can be effective
oday.

Bank, Lombard Street, London
Photo David Warner

Bank, Berkeley Square, London
Photo David Warner

Sun Life Assurance, Barbican City, London
Photo David Warner

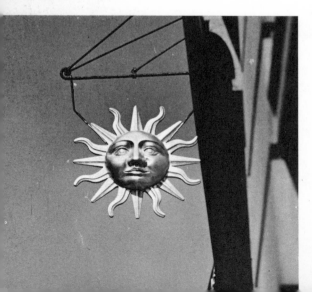

Bank, Lombard Street, London ▶
Photo David Warner

Custom Design Group, St Christopher's Place, London
Design Edward Wright

However, letterforms it must be for most jobs, evocative though hanging signs are. The following examples show what exciting solutions are produced by imaginative designers exploiting new architectural materials.

Vasa, Lowndes Street, London
Architect S. Buzas, Design Hans Schleger Associates, Photo Edgar Hyman

Experimental letters in wood
Design Edward Wright

Concrete foundation stone, Churchill College, Cambridge. *Design Edward Wright*

THIS STONE WAS LAID ON THE 14TH OCTOBER 1961 BY LORD TEDDER GCB THE CHANCELLOR OF THE UNIVERSITY

Fishmonger, Fulham Broadway, London

Fish restaurant, South Kensington, London

Pub, Stroud Green, London

Fish restaurant, South Kensington, London   *Photos David Warner*

Painted house numbers
Photo Robert Brownjohn

Exit in stone
Photo Robert Brownjohn

Laundry, Carla Ratjada, Majorca

Spoon-maker, Majorca

Cabinet-maker, Majorca ▶

Photos Herbert Spencer

Here are some earlier examples in several different materials. What looks good in one material may be quite inappropriate in another. None of these signs is architectural. They are independent of the structure and contrast with it; but they do not destroy the building, rather they enliven the street. See also previous two pages.

Butcher, Stroud Green, London
Photo David Warner

Chimney sweep, Hampstead, London
Photo David Warner

A quiet, unostentatious notice, completely right in a small residential side street. Opposite are two splendid examples of rowdy fairground baroque.

Travelling Circus
Photos David Warner

Assorted hand-drawn price tickets
Photos David Warner

Mass-produced plastic price-tags would save time, but these hand-drawn tickets, dashed off by fishmongers and barrowboys, are better advertising. Pregnant forms, bursting with life and high spirits, they beautifully suggest the generous fruits of the earth.

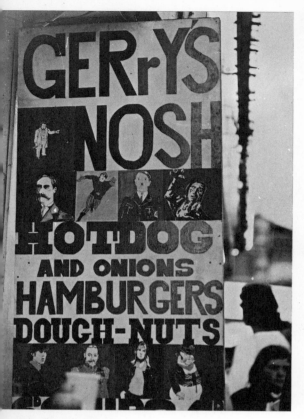

Southend on Sea
Photo David Warner

Waterloo Road, London
Photo David Warner

A sophisticated pop sign from Southend.

Two innocent signs from London and Reno.

Where the West Begins — neon sign at Reno
Photo Alan Fletcher

Travelling Circus
Photo Herbert Spencer

A magnificent sign which is just what it says.

745.3   S96s

Principles

andbook

Design

DEMCO

A